# EDUCATION LIBRARY SERVICE

## Tel: 01606 275801

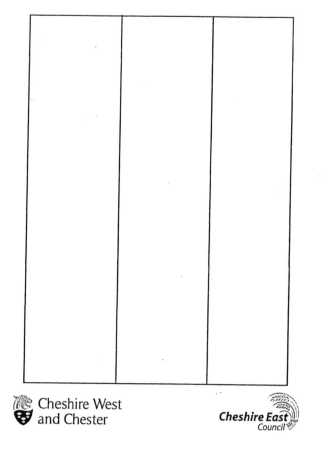

# Tumblr®:

# How David Karp Changed the Way We Blog

# WIZARDS OF TECHNOLOGY

# WIZARDS OF TECHNOLOGY

# TUMBLR®:
# How David Karp Changed the Way We Blog

## AURELIA JACKSON

Mason Crest

Mason Crest
450 Parkway Drive, Suite D
Broomall, PA 19008
www.masoncrest.com

Printed and bound in the United States of America.

First printing
9 8 7 6 5 4 3 2 1

Series ISBN: 978-1-4222-3178-4
ISBN: 978-1-4222-3186-9
ebook ISBN: 978-1-4222-8722-4

Library of Congress Cataloging-in-Publication Data

Jackson, Aurelia.
  Tumblr : how David Karp changed the way we blog / Aurelia Jackson.
      pages cm. — (Wizards of technology)
  ISBN 978-1-4222-3186-9 (hardback) — ISBN 978-1-4222-3178-4 (series) — ISBN 978-1-4222-8722-4 (ebook) 1. Karp, David, 1986- 2. Karp, David, 1986-—Juvenile literature. 3. Webmasters—United States—Biography—Juvenile literature. 4. Computer programmers—United States--Biography—Juvenile literature. 5. Tumblr (Electronic resource)—Juvenile literature. 6. Blogs—Juvenile literature. I. Title.
  TK5102.56.K37J33 2015
  338.7′61006752092—dc23
  [B]
                                        2014012232

# CONTENTS

**KEY ICONS TO LOOK FOR:**

**Text-Dependent Questions:** These questions send the reader back to the text for more careful attention to the evidence presented there.

**Words to Understand:** These words with their easy-to-understand definitions will increase the reader's understanding of the text, while building vocabulary skills.

**Series Glossary of Key Terms:** This back-of-the book glossary contains terminology used throughout this series. Words found here increase the reader's ability to read and comprehend higher-level books and articles in this field.

**Research Projects:** Readers are pointed toward areas of further inquiry connected to each chapter. Suggestions are provided for projects that encourage deeper research and analysis.

**Sidebars:** This boxed material within the main text allows readers to build knowledge, gain insights, explore possibilities, and broaden their perspectives by weaving together additional information to provide realistic and holistic perspectives.

## Words to Understand

**technology:** Things that people invent to make something easier to to do something new.

**specialized:** Got very good at one particular thing.

**animation:** The technique of combining still images to create the illusion of movement.

**mentor:** An advisor or guide, especially one with more experience.

**expertise:** Expert skill or knowledge in a certain area.

# CHAPTER ONE

# Starting Strong

David Karp came up with a great idea before he was even twenty years old. He became successful by inventing something that would improve the lives of others. He felt the Internet was missing something, and he decided to fill that gap with a type of blog that would change the way everyday people used the Internet forever. David is very young compared to most successful businessmen, but he's already earned a fortune. In fact, he is worth an estimated two hundred million dollars!

David's invention, named Tumblr, was officially released to the public in 2007. Many users were instantly hooked, and it was easy to see why.

Today, Yahoo! owns Tumblr, but David hasn't given up control of his company to the Internet giant.

David had worked hard to make a website that was easy to use while also allowing members to be creative. Users could upload text comments, photos, videos, or even voice clips to their own personal webpage without knowing anything about computer programming. To top it all, Tumblr was entirely free to use and ad-free!

Two weeks after Tumblr launched, the website had 75,000 members. After six years, the website had gained over one hundred million users with over sixty billion blog posts. Tumblr continues to grow. Tumblr, Inc. had started out as a project between David Karp and Marco Arment, but now the website employs over two hundred people.

David decided to sell Tumblr in 2013 for several reasons. One of the biggest reasons was that he needed more money to keep Tumblr running. It was impossible for David to keep up with Tumblr's enormous growth and popularity on his own. He sold the company to an even larger company called Yahoo. This company paid David over one billion dollars for the ownership of Tumblr. He will be able to keep his title as the CEO of Tumblr for as long as he wants to, according to Yahoo.

The purchase was made final on June 20, 2013. As part of the deal, David was asked to stay with the company as the chief executive office (CEO). This ensured that Tumblr would continue to develop in a way that David had imagined. His creative ideas would continue to inspire and change Tumblr for the better in the many years to come.

Tumblr was about six years old when ownership changed hands. Six years may not seem like very long, but it can feel like a lifetime when it comes to the Internet. Tumblr has changed a lot since it first began, and it still continues to change today.

David does not let the changes in ***technology*** slow down his website. As technology improves, so do the availability and many features of Tumblr. When Tumblr was first invented, for example, users could only upload posts using personal computers. Today, users can upload posts using their smartphones or tablets.

Learning how to code and create websites at an early age helped David create Tumblr later in life.

David has a lot of money, but he lives very simply. He does not own a lot of expensive clothes and does not use his money for selfish reasons. He has a sofa and one television in his apartment, which is located in Brooklyn, New York. Staying humble is very important to David because he originally developed Tumblr for everyday people.

## MAKING WEBSITES

When computers were first invented, they were very large and extremely expensive. Only the richest members of society could buy computers to call their own. All that changed around the time David Karp was born, in 1986. Computers were becoming more common both at work and at home. Some public schools even began purchasing computers for their students to use.

The personal computer is a very powerful tool. One of its most important functions in the twenty-first century is browsing the Internet. The Internet, like all inventions, began as a very small experiment. The World Wide Web was first made available to the public in the early 1990s. It started with just a few simple websites and has been expanding rapidly ever since. Society has learned to rely on the Internet in many ways. The Internet can be used to research a paper, reach out to friends, or even share ideas with the entire world.

Growing up, David was always fascinated with the Internet. Merely visiting his favorite websites was not enough for someone as clever as David, though. He wanted to make his own websites for the world to see. Back in the 1990s, there were no programs to build a website for you like the ones that exist today. It was very difficult to make a website without programming it yourself.

Computer programmers use strings of code to tell a computer what to do. Computer languages are made up of these strings of code. Learning how to make a website is a lot like learning how to speak any other new language. There are many different types of computer languages. Some are used to make programs. Others are used to build websites. The most basic computer language used to build a website is known as HTML.

HTML stands for HyperText Markup Language. Programmers use HTML code to tell a computer what to display on a website. For example, a web developer can use a special HTML command to change the color of the text shown on a website. Another command can change the background color of the page. The possibilities are endless when it comes to HTML.

David began teaching himself how to use HTML when he was eleven years old. Books and websites were a very helpful part of his research. Along with learning came experimentation. David tried his hand at building websites and realized he liked it a lot. He was creating websites of his very own before he could drive!

At the time, David was attending classes at the Calhoun School. His mother worked there as a science teacher and encouraged his interest in technology. David was a good student, but he was far more interested in his own projects than what he learned at school.

As David grew older, he knew he wanted to use his skills to become an entrepreneur. An entrepreneur is a person who starts his own business. David's first business venture, he decided, would be creating websites for small businesses. But in the meantime, he had a lot to learn.

## HIS OWN BUSINESS

David took an internship job at the age of fourteen. An intern is someone who works for very little pay, or even for free, in order to learn a job. One of the companies David worked with was Frederator Studios, which *specialized* in *animation*. The founder of the company, Fred Seibert, was a friend of David's family, and he became a *mentor* to David. He taught David a lot about computer animation and web development while David worked at the company.

David used his time at Frederator Studios to soak up all the knowledge he could from older, more experienced programmers and engineers. The employees of Frederator Studios were so impressed with David that they were part of the reason David landed his first real job. When a growing Internet forum needed help, one of David's coworkers recommended him for the job.

An Internet forum is a website where people can go to talk to one another through a string of messages known as threads. There are many different types of forums on the World Wide Web. David was asked to help develop a parenting forum named UrbanBaby. Mothers who lived in the city would visit the site to communicate with other urban mothers. David finished his first project for UrbanBaby in just a few short hours. The owners of the forum were so impressed that they hired him as a permanent employee not long after.

David had been living in New York with his family, but he spent some time in Japan while he was working for UrbanBaby. None of his coworkers knew he was in Japan or even that he was only seventeen years old until long after he moved there. They were extremely surprised when they found out David's real location and age. David worked for UrbanBaby until 2006. He left when it was sold to a much larger company.

David saw leaving UrbanBaby as an opportunity to strike out on his own. He had earned a lot of money while he was working for the company, and now he was ready to use this money to start up his very own software consultancy company. A consultant is someone who is hired on a case-by-case basis to answer questions and solve problems for clients. David's company spent a lot of his time altering software to fit a client's needs. The company David started became known as Davidville.

David's company took off during its first year. At the time, David was extremely embarrassed by his age. He thought clients would not take him seriously if they knew how young he was, so he spoke to most of his clients over the phone and tried to avoid meeting them in person. He lied about his age and time in the industry during phone interviews, always saying that he was older and more experienced than he actually was.

When David created and launched Tumblr, he was still a young man in his early twenties.

## Make Connections

David spent a year at a high school specializing in science before dropping out. He started being homeschooled soon after while working on his computer projects at home. This was around the same time he began working for UrbanBaby. David planned to earn his high school diploma and eventually go to college, but his plan changed once his company became successful. It was so successful, in fact, that David saw no reason to go back to high school. He became a success without ever graduating from high school.

David's plan to keep his real identity a secret worked, and most of his clients never questioned him or his ***expertise***.

Companies that are doing well sometimes decide to expand. An expanding company may hire new employees or move to a bigger office. David decided to expand by hiring someone to be his business partner. Marco Arment was a talented engineer who could help turn David's dreams into reality. Within just one year, David and Marco would develop and release one of the most powerful blogging websites on the Internet.

## BLOGS

Just one hundred years ago, almost everything we needed to learn came directly from printed material. Students and teachers used books, newspapers, and magazines to learn about the world. The rise of the Internet, however, forever changed the way we exchange information. Students no longer need to take a trip to the library to research a topic. Instead,

Marco Arment helped David make Tumblr into the success it is today.

## Make Connections

German designer Chris Neukirchen first used the term "Tumblin". Some of the first two Tumblelogs were known as Anarchaia and Projectionist.

they can log online and visit a number of reliable research websites from the comfort of their homes or classrooms.

The Internet is one of the fastest ways to share information with people from all over the world. One of the ways people share information is through blogs. The word "blog" is a shortened form of the word "we-blog," which was a term first invented in 1997.

People make blogs for all sorts of reasons. Some blogs act as personal online journals or diaries. Others are used to help other people. A cooking blog might teach viewers how to make certain dishes. A blog about technology will keep track of all the new developments in the world of science. Sometimes, blogs follow the latest trends in the media. There are blogs devoted to upcoming movies, television shows, and even bands.

Blogs were increasing in popularity when David began his own company in 2006. Like many people his age, David tried starting a few blogs of his own. He found that he did not like the type of blogs that already existed. They were meant for long, detailed posts. David preferred writing short posts that were only a few sentences long.

David learned about a special type of blogging platform known as tumblelogs. Tumblelogs are short-form blogs and are included in a

## Text-Dependent Questions

1. The author gives several reasons for why Tumblr has become so popular. What are they?
2. What are three examples of the Internet's many uses listed by the author at the beginning of the chapter?
3. What does HTML stand for and what is it used for?
4. Where did the term blog come from? List three different types of blogs you might find on the Internet.
5. What is a Tumblelog? How is it different from other blog types?

category of blogs known as microblogs. The only rule for tumblelogs is that they can only be a few sentences long. In other words, they were the exact type of blog David wanted to use.

David could not find a tumblelog, however, that exactly fit his needs. A popular tumblelog site that was easy to use had not been invented yet. All the most popular blogging sites catered to people who wrote long blog posts. Two websites that were popular blogging sites at the time were Blogger and Wordpress. Davidville hosted its company blog on Wordpress until 2008.

David saw an opportunity when he realized there were not many tumblelog websites. He believed that a website featuring tumblelogs would be incredibly popular, and he knew it was only a matter of time before one was created by someone else. He waited over a year, but to his amazement, not a single person had invented a tumblelog site. David realized that if he wanted to use a website dedicated to tumblelogs, he would have to create one himself.

## Research Project

Tumblr is only one example of a blogging website. Using the Internet, research and write about at least three other blogging websites that are popular today. List the similarities and differences between these other websites and Tumblr. Finally, which blogging website would you prefer to use and why?

David and his partner Marco set to work and developed Tumblr. David became the chief executive officer (CEO), while Marco became the chief technology officer (CTO). The website was first created in February of 2007, but David and Marco could tell that it still needed a lot of work before it was ready to go live. They worked tirelessly over many months to get the website ready for the public. Soon, though, their big idea would go live!

## Words to Understand

***customized:*** Made unique, for a certain person.
***profit:*** Money that you make after all expenses have been paid.

# CHAPTER TWO

# Listening to the Users

Most web developers do not make something amazing on their first try. It took David three tries and almost a full year to build a website that was well received by the public. David and Marco listened to the concerns of all the people who tried the earlier versions of Tumblr before they released Version 3.0. This version was far more user friendly than any other versions, and it offered plenty of new features that the previous versions did not have.

## SUCCESS!

Tumblr officially launched in November 2007. David could immediately tell that Tumblr was going to be successful from this point forward. New

David worked hard to put all of his knowledge about making websites into Tumblr, focusing on making the website easy to use.

users were signing up by the thousands each day. Over 75,000 users signed up within the first two weeks of the third version's launch.

David was so overwhelmed by his newfound success that he was forced to choose between Tumblr and his consultancy business. He simply did not have the time or money to manage both. David kept Marco as his partner and renamed Davidville. The new company was Tumblr, Inc.

David is extremely tech-savvy, which means he has no problem picking up a new machine or website and using it right away. Even the most complicated websites are easy for someone like David to navigate. Now, David had two goals in mind for Tumblr.

His first goal was to create a website that was easy for everyone to use. He had clearly succeeded in that goal. Even signing up and logging in takes very little effort. One of Tumblr's selling points is that users can post their first entry in just a few short minutes.

David's second goal was this: he wanted to create a website where a user could create unique posts for the entire world to see. David wanted his website to encourage users' creativity.

## EASY TO USE

Tumblr has changed a lot over the years, but its basic features still remain the same. Going to Tumblr.com reveals a simple login screen with a random user-posted image in the background. The first thing users see once they log in is what Tumblr refers to as "the dashboard." This is similar to the dashboard of a car because it shows all the most important information in a simple format. David sees no reason to complicate the Tumblr experience with extra buttons or tabs.

The very top of the dashboard allows users to make a post. The options for what users will post about are nearly endless. They might make a short text entry, link a website, post a video, or even share a picture. It is also possible to post quotes. Most posts are short and to the point, just like on other tumblelog websites. Users are not pressured to make

David shows off Tumblr in New York City in 2007.

large entries, which makes them more likely to post on Tumblr than other blogging sites.

All the features included in the final version of Tumblr were aimed at one thing: exposure. Tumblr remained a step ahead of other tumblelog websites by allowing users to interact with one another in a number of different ways. User interaction is one of the basic features of all social media websites, including Facebook and Twitter. One of the ways to interact with another user on Tumblr is by "following" that person. For example, if you stumble upon a post you like and want to see more like it, you have the option to "follow" the user who posted it. Following a user ensures that you will see all future updates from that person.

Who you follow is entirely up to you. It could be a friend, a famous celebrity, or simply someone who posts ideas you find interesting. Posts from people you follow are displayed on another area of the dashboard. If you ever decide you don't want to follow a person anymore, simply delete that user from the list of people you follow.

User interaction does not end with following each other. Another way users can interact is by supporting each other's posts. There are two ways to support a post you like. The first way is by "liking" it. There is a button beneath every post on Tumblr shaped like a heart. If a user clicks on this button, the post gains one "like." Posts with a lot of likes are more likely to be seen by other users on Tumblr.

The second, and more important, way to support a post is by "reblogging" it. If users click the "reblog" button on the bottom of a post, that post will be copied and posted on the users' own pages for all to see. Users reblogging posts also have the option to type a comment below the original posts. This is an effective way to let other users know what they think about the original post.

## AN OUTLET FOR CREATIVITY

David was practically an expert at designing websites by the time he started working on Tumblr. After all, he had been practicing since he was

Tumblr made sharing photos easy and fun. People taking photos of their friends or professional photographers could share their shots with a huge number of Tumblr users.

## Make Connections

One of the ways users can customize Tumblr is by using something known as a "theme." Themes are prebuilt webpage designs that users can customize however they want. Some themes are free to use while others cost money. As of 2013, the most expensive theme can be bought for $49.

just a little kid. So it's no surprise that David easily succeeded in meeting his first goal of making an easy-to-use tumblelog website. His second goal would not be as easy to accomplish. It was far more complicated to create.

At the time of Tumblr's creation, there were not a lot of easy ways for people to share their creativity with others on the Internet. Other social media sites like Facebook and Twitter could not be **customized**. Users could post text and images, but that was it. They could not create a unique user page to call their own.

Tumblr became one of the first websites to give users the option to be as creative as they wanted to be with their homepage. Every single part of a user's page can be changed, from the way posts are displayed to the pictures shown in the background. The font types and colors can be easily altered, too. Users do not need to know anything about building a website to customize a Tumblr page.

Customizable pages were only the beginning when it came to allowing Tumblr's users to be creative. David made sure that all creative users would have a way to share their work. With the official launch of Tumblr came the ability for artists to post any photographs they have taken. Short poetry can be posted on Tumblr, too. Musicians can post audio clips to

Tumblr helped musicians, poets, and painters reach new fans online.

give fans a previews of their latest music. Animated images, known as GIFs, are also extremely popular on Tumblr.

Tumblr isn't just for artists, however. Fans of any sort of hobby can find a way to express their likes and dislikes on Tumblr. Lovers of history may wish to post quotes from favorite historical figures. Media buffs could post and discuss the latest movie trailer to an upcoming movie. David wanted Tumblr to become a place for everyone, and he succeeded in achieving this goal.

## SELLING TO INVESTORS

In just one short year, Tumblr became extremely successful. It was estimated at a worth of about $3 million dollars, but David was having trouble keeping up in more ways than just one. The workload involved in maintaining and updating the website was simply too much for himself and Marco to handle. They knew it was only a matter of time before they had to hire more employees.

One of the biggest draws of Tumblr is that it is completely free to use. David intended to keep it that way. Unfortunately, running a website costs money, and Tumblr was growing much faster than anyone could have guessed. The servers, or computers that hosted Tumblr's website, were becoming crowded. It was hard for the website to stay connected to thousands of users at a time. The only way to fix this problem would be to upgrade the servers.

David and Marco knew they needed to reach out for more money and resources. In October 2008, they decided to sell 25 percent of Tumblr to wealthy investors in October of 2008. Investors are people who give money to a company in order to help it succeed. Should the company become successful, investors will receive some of the company's *profit*. Investors will lose money if the company does not do well.

David was originally offered over one million dollars to sell half his company, but he declined because he knew that would mean giving up control of the company David and Marco had worked so hard to build.

## Research Project

Using the Internet, research and find five big companies that currently use Tumblr. List these companies and explain how having a Tumblr account helps each of these companies communicate with their customers.

Selling just 25 percent ensured that David would retain creative control over the company. However, the investors now had a say in how he used their money.

The extra money from selling part of the company was what he needed to make his company grow even larger. David had hopes of reaching one million unique users by the end of 2008.

At the end of 2008, David estimated that Tumblr, Inc., would have enough money run the website for just over one more year. After that, the company would have to start finding still more ways to raise money. David came up with two possible ways the company could make extra money.

The first would be through a voluntary, paid "premium" membership for users. A user who paid for a premium membership would have access to extra features that the unpaid Tumblr user would not have. However, users who did not pay would still be allowed to use the Tumblr service for free. Some websites, including a photography website known as Flickr, offered similar options at the time.

A second way David could bring in money for the company would be through advertising. Companies would pay Tumblr to put advertisements on user pages. Tumblr would be paid based on how many users saw the ads and clicked on them. A popular page like Tumblr would be able to

## Text-Dependent Questions

1. Which version of Tumblr was released in November of 2007? What made it different from the previous versions of Tumblr?
2. How does Tumblr allow users to support each other?
3. What were the two goals David had in mind when creating Tumblr? Did he succeed in meeting those goals?
4. What percent of the company did David sell at the end of 2008? Why did he choose to sell this percent instead of a larger percent?

make a lot of money that way. Unfortunately, ads do have a downside. Users would not be happy about seeing ads all the time, so David chose to keep his page ad-free for the time being.

He was determined to keep Tumblr growing, though. David knew he would have to come up with new ideas to make that happen.

# Words to Understand

**hosting:** Storing a website on servers for people to access over the Internet.

**trends:** The general directions being taken by fashions or the other things people like.

**categorize:** Put in a certain group.

# CHAPTER THREE

# Keeping Up

David knows that the world of technology is constantly changing. Change can bring either big problems or big opportunities—and David is determined to turn each new technological development into an opportunity for Tumblr to grow. He understands that if he wants his company to keep up, he has to be ready to help Tumblr adapt and change.

## SMARTPHONES

Tumblr was first released in a time when smartphones were becoming very popular. The main difference between normal cellphones and smartphones is the smartphone's ability to launch applications, or apps. There are all sorts of apps for smartphones. Some apps help a user navigate

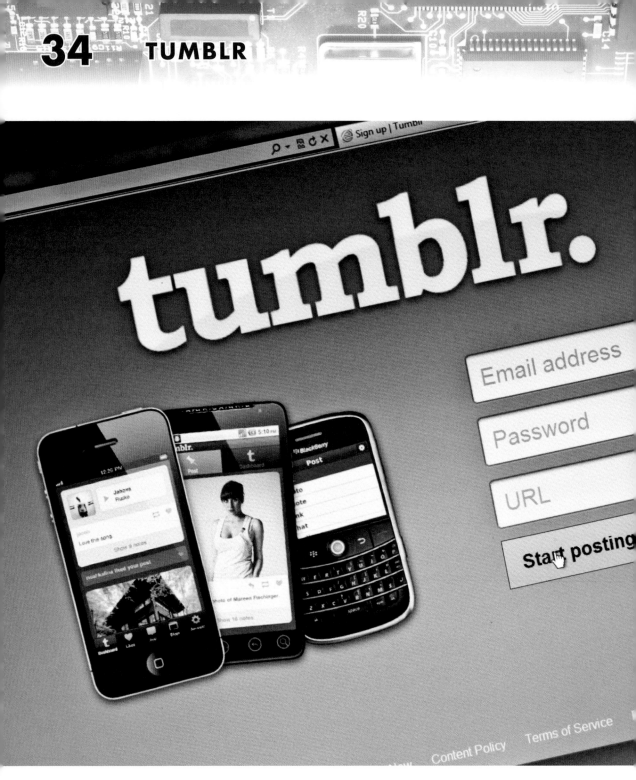

David made sure that Tumblr created smartphone apps as mobile devices became more popular with users.

## Make Connections

Marco Arment began his own business venture in 2008 when he founded Instapaper. This is a service that allows users to bookmark and save any webpage to their Instapaper account. The user can then go back to the account at a later date and read any unread pages. It is most useful when the user has more than one device. He or she might save the page while using a smartphone and then view it later on a computer. Marco left Tumblr in 2010 so that he could focus on Instapaper.

from one location to another. Others help a user find a place to eat lunch. Many apps are used for social media sites such as Facebook, Twitter, and Tumblr.

The original iPhone was released in 2007, the same year Tumblr was released. David was a big fan of the iPhone, and he was very excited when he found out a Tumblr app was being released for the iPhone. Developers Jeff Rock and Garrett Ross originally created the iPhone app, known as Tumblerette. It cost $1.99 to buy and was very easy to use.

Tumblr bought Tumblerette and made it the official Tumblr app in 2009. This was a turning point for Tumblr because the app became free to use and was downloadable by anyone with an iPhone. Tumblr apps for the Android and Blackberry phones were released in 2010. Two years later, Tumblr released an application for the Windows phone as well.

All Tumblr posts once needed to be posted directly from the Tumblr website. With the introduction of the Tumblr app, users could post from anywhere cellphone reception is available. All it takes is a click of a button. Smartphones are becoming more popular with each coming year, so having a working smartphone app helped Tumblr become one of the most used sites on the Internet.

With Tumblr's smartphone apps, users can upload photos no matter where they are.

Tumblr usage continued to increase dramatically. About twenty million users were visiting Tumblr each day at the start of 2010. That number grew to fifty million by the end of the year, and doubled to one hundred million before 2012 even began. The mobile users per day also increased, with the most mobile users visiting the website in 2013. This number is expected to climb as smartphones become even more common.

## INTRODUCING ADVERTISEMENTS

2012 marked another big year for Tumblr. The website was receiving so many visits a day that it was ranked one of the top-ten visited websites in the United States, as measured by Quantcast. The amount of visits a website receives a day is known as web traffic. A website can keep track of its success based on how much traffic it gets per day.

But Tumblr needed more money to keep its success going. The website was also getting too large for David to manage alone. He was forced to hire employees to help him keep Tumblr going strong. Unfortunately, this meant that he needed to find a way to pay his new employees.

Another reason David needed money was to help pay for the website's bandwidth usage. Bandwidth is the measurement of how much data—or information—is transferred over a network. In other words, a website's used bandwidth is the amount of information transferred to the millions of users constantly accessing the Tumblr website. Transferred bandwidth is not free, and Tumblr must pay the company *hosting* the website to handle it.

David was already making some money through the premium themes sold on Tumblr, but it was not enough to keep the website afloat. A website as large and powerful as Tumblr costs millions of dollars to run each year. By the end of 2012, Tumblr, Inc., had spent over twenty-five million dollars to manage the website and pay employees. It was estimated that Tumblr would need to spend even more money in the year 2013. David would have to find a way to come up with the extra money if his website was going to survive.

While many technology companies call California home, Tumblr's offices are in New York City.

The easiest way to both pay his employees and keep Tumblr going would be to start selling advertisement space. Up until that point, Tumblr was free to use and had absolutely no ads. Users were understandably upset when advertisements began showing up on the website, but they couldn't have been surprised by the change. Facebook and Twitter had recently introduced paid advertisements as well.

David explained the type of advertisements that would appear on Tumblr during an interview in April 2013. While other websites used simple text and link advertisements, David wanted Tumblr ads to be more creative than that. People who make advertisements would finally have a place to show off their creative side. Tumblr allows larger, more engaging advertisements that users will be more likely to interact with and pay attention to.

One of the first companies Tumblr partnered with to host advertisements was Adidas. Adidas is a sporting company, and it chose to start a soccer blog on Tumblr in addition to the advertisements the company paid for. All Adidas advertisements showed up on a user's dashboard. They didn't stop a user from posting, but they could not be ignored.

Some other companies have been following Adidas' lead starting in 2012. A growing business can use Tumblr as a free and popular way to keep in touch with customers. Newspapers and television stations are just two examples of the many companies that now post on Tumblr regularly. Users who follow these companies can repost or respond to questions posted by these companies with one click of a button. The most urgent news stories can spread around the Internet in a matter of minutes.

## CHANGING TRENDS

When comes to the Internet, new *trends* are constantly emerging. Social networks around the world were forced to change starting in 2009 when the short-form blogging website known as Twitter introduced hashtag support. Hashtags allow users to *categorize* their posts. Other users can search for similar posts by searching for a certain hashtag. A

Twitter's use of hashtags has spread to a number of social networking sites, including Tumblr.

hashtag is made up of a pound sign and a word. One example would be: #tumblr.

It was only a matter of time before other websites followed suit. Instagram, an image website, started using hashtags in 2011. Google+ also began recognizing hashtags, and 2013 marked the year Facebook and Flickr officially embraced the hashtag. Many of the newest websites are now launched with hashtag support built in. As much as 70 percent of hashtags are used while a user is on a mobile app. The other 30 percent are used on a personal computer.

Tumblr now allows users to tag posts. All the user has to do is type a word into the "tag" box when a post is being made. That word can then be linked and searched for by other users. Tags are one more way users can connect with each other when using Tumblr. It was not a part of the website when Tumblr first launched, but it is now a widely used feature.

One of the newest trends of social networking websites is the ability to link one of your accounts with accounts from other popular websites. Tumblr hasn't been left out of this trend. It is now fully linked with Facebook, meaning that any post made on Tumblr can be automatically posted directly to a user's Facebook page with the click of a button. This feature is extremely convenient for people who use both websites. A Tumblr user no longer needs to copy and paste the same entry in two places.

## NO ONE'S PERFECT!

David's many good decisions led Tumblr to become the blogging giant it is today. But, like all company owners, David made a few mistakes along the way. One mistake was creating a special feature known as the "Storyboard." It was launched in May 2012 and was managed by a group of editors and journalists who worked for Tumblr, Inc. The point of "Storyboard" was to introduce Tumblr users to blogs that the typical user might not normally see. It was one of the ways Tumblr tried to encourage and support creativity.

Tumblr and Facebook are different, but the two competing social networks have had similar problems when it comes to introducing new features.

The stories featured on Storyboard varied, but one thing remained the same: an editorial team chose every featured story. Videos were also occasionally posted about famous Tumblr bloggers.

Tumblr was not the first website to feature a program like Storyboard. Facebook had tried a similar approach, but that program was eventually shut down. Programs like Storyboard simply weren't what the users of Facebook and Tumblr wanted.

Storyboard lasted for just over a year before it was discontinued. David chose to end the program because he realized it wasn't working. He learned from his mistake. He has said that he will not launch another program like "Storyboard" in the future.

## RESPECTING PRIVACY

David needed to make Tumblr friendly for all members if it was going to become one of the most used blogging platforms on the Internet. He did this by limiting the amount of information Tumblr asks when a person signs up. Users are allowed to keep their real lives separate from their online identity. Tumblr does not ask users to give a real name, unlike other social networking sites like Facebook and Google+. Tumblr users are not asked to post information about where they went to school, where they live, or whom they are related to. All this information can be kept private.

People who use Tumblr only share as much as they want to share with the world. Tumblr users can be as anonymous as they want to be, which allows them to be creative if they so choose. It is also possible to change the privacy of each post a user makes. A user can post or repost something to his or her blog while preventing everyone else from seeing it. How Tumblr is used depends entirely on the user. To one user, a Tumblr page may act as a private diary. To another, it could be a very public blog.

## KEEPING PEOPLE INTERESTED

Another way David increased the total number of Tumblr users was by keeping the current users engaged. Some Tumblr users post multiple times a day. Others don't post as often because they simply don't know what to talk about. Tumblr helps these users find their voice by offering question prompts through an automated robot known as Tumblrbot. Every so often, a question will show up in a user's inbox. The user can answer this question or ignore it.

Another way to ask or answer questions is through the use of the built in "ask me anything" page. This page can be enabled in a user's blog settings. Anyone with this page enabled can be asked questions by other users. There is also an option to allow anonymous questions. The "ask me anything" feature is a fun way for people to get to know each other. Users who do not wish to be asked questions can simply disable this page, which makes it impossible for any questions to be asked.

## Research Project

Using the Internet, research and find how many employees are currently employed directly by Tumblr. How has that number changed since the company first started in 2007? Do you feel the total number of employees will increase or decrease over the next couple of years? Explain your reasoning.

Another feature added to Tumblr to keep people interested in the website is the ability to delay posts. This allows users to set a time for a post to be added to their Tumblr page. This feature is especially useful for people who do not have a lot of time on their hands. Companies who use Tumblr might find this feature useful because it allows announcements to be made right at midnight without an employee manually adding a post.

David has done a lot to build his company. He's brought it a long way in just a few short years. Now he has to make sure Tumblr has what it takes for the future.

# Words to Understand

**personalized:** Made specifically for a certain person.
**accuracy:** How precise something is, or how close to being correct it is.

# CHAPTER FOUR

# The Future of Tumblr

The year 2013 started off well for David and his company. Paid advertisements were bringing in a lot of money, and Tumblr was growing as fast as ever.

At just twenty-six years of age, David was not experienced, however, at leading a company with over a hundred employees. It was an exciting new challenge, but not something he wanted to be doing forever. Offers to buy the company began rolling in. One of the most tempting offers came from Yahoo!.

Many of Tumblr's users were worried about David selling his company to Yahoo!, but David was sure he was making the right decision.

Tumblr wouldn't be moving into the Yahoo! offices, and David would be keeping control over his company.

## SALE TO YAHOO

David's plan to sell Tumblr to Yahoo! was first made public on May 20, 2013. Many fans of Tumblr were not happy about the news. They feared that once a large company took over, Tumblr would stop being the creative outlet it had always been. Users were so upset that a petition was started. The goal of the petition was to stop David and Tumblr, Inc., from selling the company. One petition on ipetitions.com received over 170,000 signatures.

David has made Tumblr into a huge success. Today, the website is used by millions of people, including the rich and famous.

## Make Connections

Tumblr originally started as a blogging platform for everyday users. It has become so popular that it now pulls members from all walks of life. Famous musicians, comedians, and even movie stars use the website to communicate with fans and blog their thoughts about life. Even Barack Obama has his own Tumblr account!

What angry fans of Tumblr did not realize was that David would not be able to keep Tumblr going on his own. He had no choice but to sell ownership of his company to someone else. Yahoo! stepped up to the task and offered to buy Tumblr for over one billion dollars. The sale was finalized exactly one month after it was first announced. Tumblr, Inc., became a subsidiary of Yahoo!. (Any company that is owned by a larger company is known as a subsidiary of the larger company.)

Some Tumblr users threatened to move to another blogging site if Tumblr was sold, but not many people left after the purchase happened. The amount of unique Tumblr users has remained mostly steady since the sale took place. It is possible that Tumblr has already reached its peak of active users, but only time will tell.

The amount of money David was paid for his company might have been enough to convince any other young CEO to give up control of his company, but not David. He did not want to sell the company unless he was allowed to remain as its CEO. Luckily, Yahoo! wanted to keep David as the CEO. The company trusted his judgment. David had built Tumblr from the ground up and had helped it thrive in a changing online world. If anyone could keep Tumblr going strong, it would be him.

David has learned a lot about running a company since he launched Tumblr in 2007.

## Make Connections

One very real concern for social media sites is the security of these websites. If web programmers are not careful, the websites they work so hard to maintain will be the victims of a web attack. One attack in December 2012 forced users to repost vulgar images and text without their consent. Tumblr quickly fixed the problem. The virus was blocked from affecting others, but not before as many as eight thousand unique blog accounts were infected.

## STATISTICS

Tumblr has continued to grow in size and popularity since it began. The website has an impressive amount of unique users. As of November 2013, Tumblr hosts over 147 million blogs. The amount of total blog posts is even higher, at over sixty-seven billion. This means that there are about 454 blog posts for every one Tumblr user. Of course, not all users will make that many posts, but many others will post much more than that!

In 2013, David announced that the average Tumblr user will spend more time on Tumblr than any other website. Recent studies show that the average user that logs into Tumblr will spend over twenty minutes on Tumblr each day. This is slightly higher than the average Facebook or Twitter user. Tumblr users are most active during the weekend and at night. Forty-two percent of all activity happens within the span of eight hours, between 5:00 p.m. and 1:00 a.m. This suggests that many Tumblr users browse Tumblr as a way to relax after work or school.

The majority of Tumblr users are young. In fact, 45 percent of users

Tumblr is one of the most successful Internet companies today, alongside Facebook, Twitter, and Pinterest.

### Research Project

Using the Internet, research and write about the latest social media trends of this year. What changes have occurred on social media websites since 2013? How will these changes help both companies and creative users gain the exposure they crave?

are under thirty-five years old. Tumblr has more active users between the age of thirteen and twenty-five than Facebook, its number one competitor. And just because Tumblr users are young doesn't mean they're uneducated! Over half of Tumblr users have at least a college degree, while over 60 percent of users make over $30,000 a year.

Tumblr is not just popular in the United States. In fact, it has a worldwide audience. The highest user count comes from the United States, but many users also come from Brazil, the United Kingdom, Canada, and Russia. This diverse audience makes Tumblr a great way to share information about international events. When a natural disaster happens, many users turn to Tumblr for answers. Posts added by Tumblr staff may let users know how to donate to relief funds following a hurricane, tornado, earthquake or typhoon.

## WHAT THE FUTURE HOLDS

One of the great challenges of running a growing blog website is helping users find posts that they will enjoy. As of 2013, a total of about ninety million posts are created on Tumblr each day. With so many blog posts being added each day, it would be impossible for a user to sort through every blog post alone.

Fortunately, Tumblr has ways to help users find exactly what they are looking for. Tumblr uses a combination of mathematical calculations and programs written by web programmers to do this. One way Tumblr helps users is by keeping track of every single post a user visits, likes, or reblogs. This data is then used to help Tumblr decide what the user's interests are.

A special group of Tumblr employees are in charge of looking at how someone uses Tumblr. Understanding what a user visits allows these staff members to improve which posts Tumblr will suggest for that user in the future. For example, a person who likes cooking blogs may also like restaurant blogs, but that doesn't mean all people who like cooking posts will want to see restaurant posts.

Tumblr starts learning about a user from the first time he or she visits the website and never stops collecting information for as long as that user has an account. Users who spend a lot of time on Tumblr will have the most *personalized* suggestions. The *accuracy* of the tools used to detect a user's interests continues to improve with each passing day. David and his team work tirelessly to make sure of it.

While it would be impossible to predict what the trends of the future will be, one thing is certain: David Karp and Tumblr, Inc. will keep up with whatever new features are added to other websites. David's creativity and drive have brought the company a long way—and he's not about to give up now!

# FIND OUT MORE

## In Books

Jenkins, Sue. *Tumblr for Dummies.* Hoboken, N.J.: John Wiley & Sons, 2012.

Kenney, Karen Latchana. *David Karp: The Mastermind Behind Tumblr.* Minneapolis, Minn.: Lerner Publications, 2013.

Rosenberg, Scott. *Say Everything: How Blogging Began, What It's Becoming, and Why It Matters.* New York: Three Rivers, 2009.

Selfridge, Benjamin, and Peter Selfridge. *A Kid's Guide to Creating Web Pages for Home and School.* Chicago, Ill.: Zephyr, 2004.

Topper, Hilary. *Everything You Ever Wanted to Know about Social Media, but Were Afraid to Ask.* Bloomington, Ind.: Iuniverse, 2009.

## On the Internet

Daily Dot: "The Real Origins of Tumblr"
www.dailydot.com/business/origin-tumblr-anarchaia-projectionist-david-karp

The Guardian: "David Karp, Founder of Tumblr, on Realising His Dream"
www.theguardian.com/media/2012/jan/29/tumblr-david-karp-interview

Mashable: "Users Stay Longer on Tumblr Than Facebook, Says David Karp"
mashable.com/2013/04/17/users-stay-longer-on-tumblr-than-facebook

Observer: "Would You Take a Tumblr with This Man?"
observer.com/2008/01/would-you-take-a-tumblr-with-this-man

Tumblr
www.tumblr.com

# SERIES GLOSSARY
# OF KEY TERMS

**application:** A program that runs on a computer or smartphone. People often call these "apps."

**bug:** A problem with how a program runs.

**byte:** A unit of information stored on a computer. One byte is equal to eight digits of binary code—that's eight 1s or 0s.

**cloud:** Data and apps that are stored on the Internet instead of on your own computer or smartphone are said to be "in the cloud."

**data:** Information stored on a computer.

**debug:** Find the problems with an app or program and fix them.

**device:** Your computer, smartphone, or other piece of technology. Devices can often access the Internet and run apps.

**digital:** Having to do with computers or stored on a computer.

**hardware:** The physical part of a computer. The hardware is made up of the parts you can see and touch.

**memory:** Somewhere that a computer stores information that it is using.

**media:** Short for multimedia, it's the entertainment or information that can be stored on a computer. Examples of media include music, videos, and e-books.

**network:** More than one computer or device connected together so information can be shared between them.

**pixel:** A dot of light or color on a digital display. A computer monitor or phone screen has lots of pixels that work together to create an image.

**program:** A collection of computer code that does a job.

**software:** Programs that run on a computer.

**technology:** Something that people invent to make a job easier or do something new.

# INDEX

## ABOUT THE AUTHOR

**Aurelia Jackson** is a writer living and working in New York City. She has a passion for writing and a love of education, both of which she brings to all the work she does.

## PICTURE CREDITS

**Dreamstime.com:**
  6: Dolphfyn
  8: Daniel Draghici
  10: Spaxia
  24: Marco Arment
  26: Shannon Fagan
  28: Andrey Armyagov
  32: Viorel Dudau
  34: Sallyeva
  36: Seemitch
  40: Ivelinr
  42: Thinglass
  46: Marcel De Grijs

  48: Lucian Milasan
  49: Ken Wolter
  52: David Karp
  54: Pressureua

**Flickr.com:**
  14: Marco Arment
  16: Marco Arment
  22: Enrique Dans
  50: Enrique Dans

  38: Americasroof